BEN WICKS
MORE
LOSERS

BEN WICKS
MORE
LOSERS

McCLELLAND AND STEWART

Copyright © 1982 by Ben Wicks

All rights reserved. The use of any part of this publication reproduced, transmitted in any form or by any means, electronic, mechanical, photocopying, recording, or otherwise, or stored in a retrieval system, without the prior consent of the publisher is an infringement of the copyright law.

The Canadian Publishers
McClelland and Stewart Limited
25 Hollinger Road
Toronto M4B 3G2

Canadian Cataloguing in Publication Data

Wicks, Ben, 1926-
   More losers

ISBN 0-7710-8969-4

1. Losers – Anecdotes, facetiae, satire, etc.
I. Title.

PN6321.F28W53   C811.5402   C82-094567-6

Printed and bound in Canada by
T. H. Best Printing Company Limited

FOR ME
MUM

Contents

Introduction/11

Losers in Love/13

A Sporting Chance/29

The Care and Feeding of Losers/36

On the Road/40

The Body Count/45

The Moment of Truth/51

A Loser in the Family/54

Crime/58

Dumb Animals/81

...On With the Show/86

And If Elected.../99

Lambs to the Slaughter/102

Losers at Large/107

Help Wanted/115

A Dead Loss/123

BEN WICKS MORE LOSERS

Introduction

On the occasion of this, the publication of a second book of losers, it was my hope to have a person of international fame write an introduction.

Unfortunately I do not know a person of international fame sufficiently well to ask him to undertake such a task.

This is not to suggest I do not have friends. It's just that I do not have friends of international, national, or even local fame who wish to be associated with this book.

It therefore falls on my shoulders to lead you into another collection of losers of the world. I would like to be able to tell you that, since filling one book with losers, the filling of another was an impossible task. Unfortunately this was not the case. Losers breed like rabbits and the only difficulty in assembling a book like this is knowing who to leave out.

For the true losers of the world continue on their unmerry way as we see in this advertisement from the *Khalee Times*:

A lady medical graduate from India with three years gynaecology and obstetrics seeks suitable opening.

Or the weathermen in the Shetland Islands who felt that a recent gust of wind measuring 204 MPH may have broken all records. They could not be sure because a stronger gust blew away the recording equipment.

But before you point the finger, remember, we're all losers – some are just bigger losers than others. But don't despair. Things could be worse. You aren't in this book – or are you?

Losers in Love

For the lucky ones, it's love that makes the world go round. For others, the thud of a cupid's arrow in the chest can make perfectly healthy humans lose all control:

On New Year's Eve, Willier Franks was hit on the back of the head by a rock thrown by his girlfriend. "It was not the first time. The man's arms and upper body show sixteen scars from knives and other weapons wielded by the woman," the court was told yesterday. Franks now realizes there is no chance of getting this relationship off the ground.
(*The Northern Echo*)

When his woman friend suddenly walked out on him, a man kicked in the glass of a shop door and then went home and turned upside down.
(*Tiverton Gazette*)

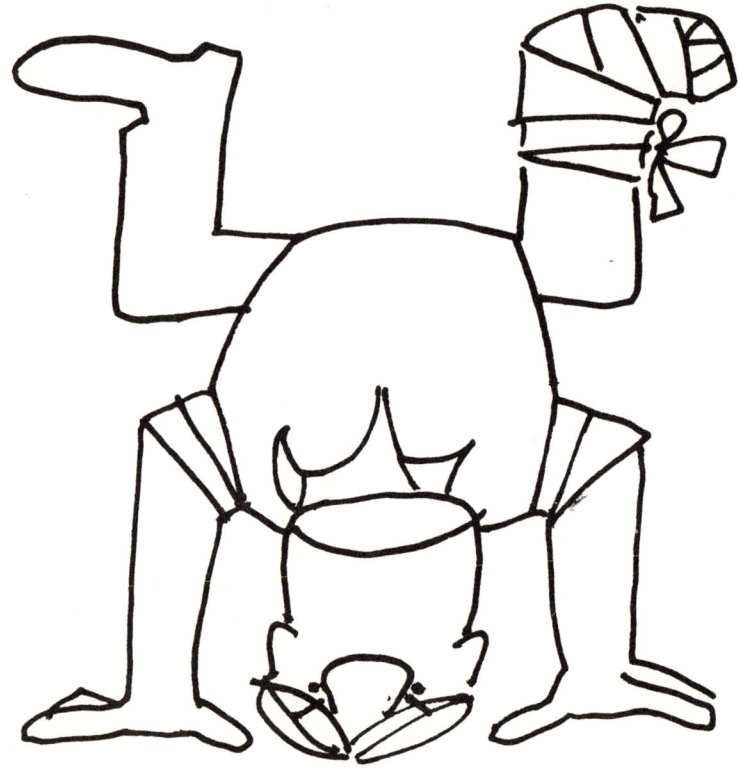

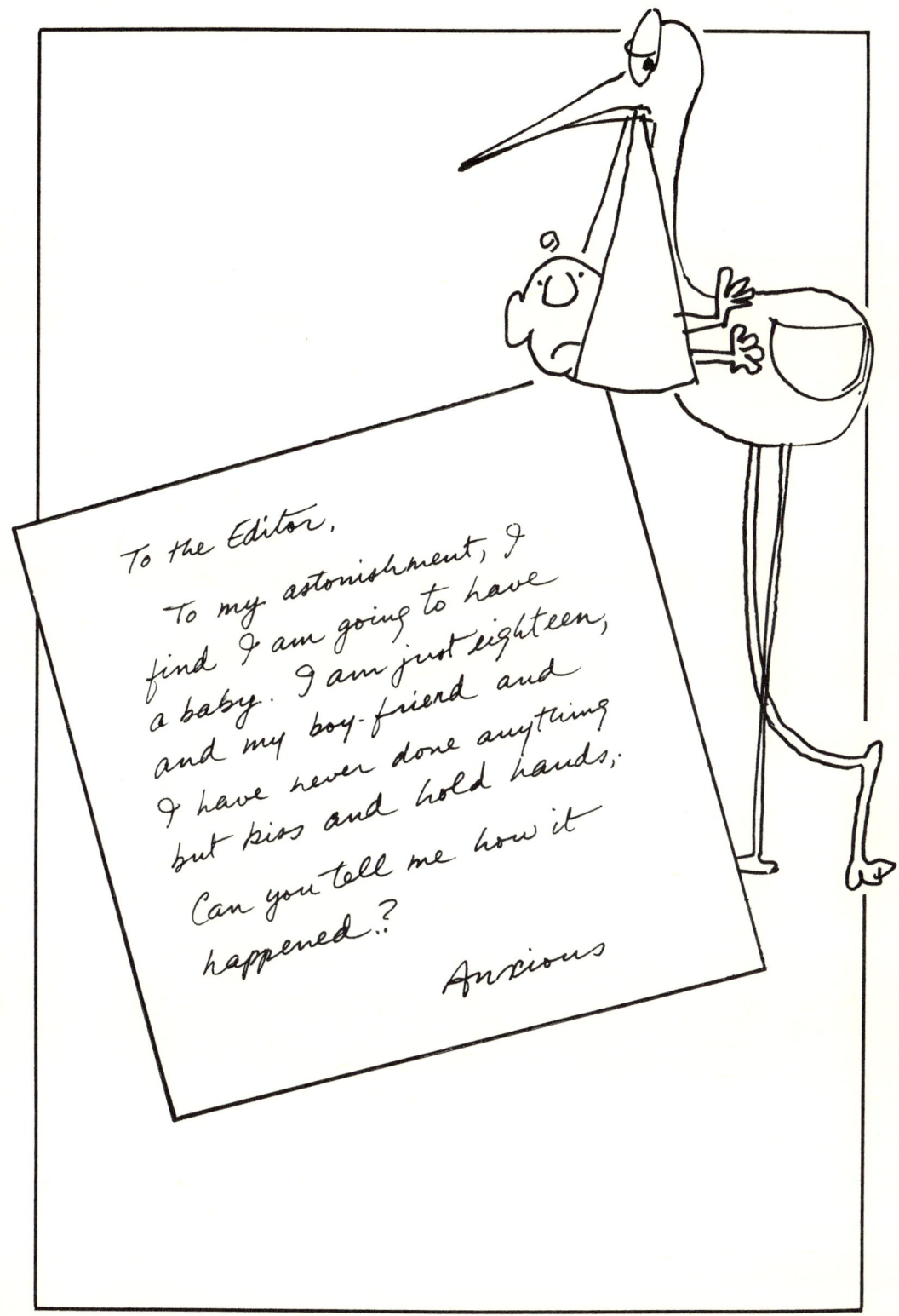

She was adventurous in her sex life, and as far as she was concerned "anything goes." However, she had not yet taken part in an orgy. She said, "Orgies were not popular in Hong Kong because it was impossible to find enough space to stage one." (*South China Post*)

He pretended his car had broken down, and persuaded her to remove her bra for him to fix the car with.
(*Wolverhampton Express and Star*)

On going to bed at night the hair should be brushed thoroughly, arranged comfortably, and carefully in case a burglar, a fireman, or a policeman visits. They are all men, too, you know, and should be considered. (Letter to the *Daily Sketch*)

Dr. Solway realized that his relationship with Mrs. Bowman was ending the day her Dobermann bit him. Instead of becoming angry with the dog, Mrs. Bowman hit Dr. Solway with a chain.
(*The Globe and Mail*)

McNicoll testified, "She knocked me over with the pram and then hit me on the head with a No Waiting sign. This is what happens every time I see her."
(*Evening News*)

A police spokesman said, "We thought the man was a terrorist the minute we heard he was carrying a sub-machine gun. Once fully mounted, these weapons are three feet long and extremely dangerous. We think it may have been a lovers' tiff."
(*Worcester Source*)

For seven hours a man defied police from a sixty-foot-high roof. Then they brought in a woman and child to help persuade him down. She called to him, "Come down, pet, I love you." But when the man still refused, she called, "Jump, then, you bloody idiot, and let's get home."
(*Scottish Express*)

I fell in love with my husband simply because he was so different from every other boy I had met. He did not like love-making and neither did I. He has never actually told me he loves me. Now, after twenty-six years of marriage, I sometimes wonder if I have missed something, but I am happy. He is a wonderful husband. He never actually proposed, but we saw a three-piece suit we liked and that clinched the idea. (Letter in the *Daily Herald*)

My husband is a jolly good sort, one of those very hearty men. He wears plus-fours, smokes a long pipe, and talks about nothing but beer and Rugby football. My nerves won't stand much more of it. (*Daily Mail*)

When my husband reads in bed on warm nights he puts a colander over his head. He says it keeps off the flies, shades his eyes from the light, and lets in air at the same time.
(Letter in *Good Shopping*)

Stepping over a pile of cats playing on the floor of her sitting-room, fifty-two-year-old Mrs. Payne said, "The trouble is that Cyril prefers animals to humans. I do not think I would have minded so much if he collected other women the way most men do." (*Sunday Express*)

The Committee records the instance of a man who wished to take divorce proceedings, but later withdrew the application "in case his wife got to hear about it." (*Annual Report, 1947,* of the Law Society)

My husband is a shy man, and whenever he brings flowers home to me he always conceals them under his hat. As a result, they have to be little flowers like violets or anemones and tend to smell of brilliantine. Surely there must be some other way in which self-conscious men cope with this problem?
(Letter in *Today*)

My bridegroom's first words to me when I joined him at the altar were, "Who are you?" It made me think that the hours I spent on myself before going to church were all worthwhile. (Letter in the *Daily Mirror*)

On her 107th birthday, in August, she attributed her great age to a lifetime of hard work and the fact that she never had a boy-friend. (*Star*)

I've been going steady with my boy-friend for two years. We're both nineteen. He says he'll never marry a girl who's not a virgin, so to be sure that I am one, he wants to have intercourse with me before we become engaged. (Letter in *Woman's Own*)

On January 26th, Elvis proposed to Ginger on his knees in the bathroom where seven months later he was found dead. "He loved to surprise me," she explained. (*Woman*)

Sex used to be treated with decent reticence; now it is discussed openly. This sort of thing can do immense harm. The moral standards accepted as "normal" by most young people today are a case in point. Why our all-wise Creator should have chosen such a distasteful – even disgusting – means of reproducing humanity is a thing that *I*, personally, have never been able to understand.
(Letter in the *Bristol Evening Post*)

The suspect told police, "I gave her a good hiding all right. I should have given her a better one. I did it because she had dyed blonde hair and I could see the roots. We are all barbarians up in Scotland. We're always getting into taxis and kicking people. Of course I hit her for nothing, but she deserved it. She gave me no reason whatsoever." (*Hartlepool Mail*)

Turned away from his wife's bingo evening because he had no card, Maurice Goodman went to the toilets in Salesbury's Central Car Park and then beckoned a man to follow him. (*Amesbury Journal*)

Judge Wethered granted a divorce to a man who, he said, found another man in his wife's bed, partly clothed, eating a hot lunch. (*Evening World*)

He said he was trying to get his clothes back because he was afraid his wife would become suspicious if he came home without them. (*Express and Star*)

I am engaged to a wonderful man, but lately he has become very moody and is always hitting me. He says it is nothing to what I shall get after marriage, and I must get used to being "kept under control." Please advise me: I want to marry him, but don't know how to handle the situation.
(Letter in *Woman's Own*)

Canine chastity belts are on sale at a well-known store. Part plastic shield, part leather harness, the contrivance is made in six sizes. The makers claim "maximum protection with minimum anxiety." (*Sunday Dispatch*)

Everybody should know how to perform "kiss-of-life" respiration; but it is undesirable that the method be practised freely for training purposes, says Surgeon Captain Stanley Miles, RN, in *Family Journal*, the British Medical Association magazine. (*The Times*)

During one month various adults have insulted my girl-friend and I and chased us from three shop doorways, three front gardens, and four draughty alleyways. (*Weekend Magazine*)

Mr. Ryan said, "I have always been in love with chimney pots. The old ones were things of beauty, and people now use them as umbrella stands and plant pots. Instead of railings around my yard I have a hedge of chimney pots." Mr. Ryan's affection for chimney pots is not shared by his wife.
(*Yorkshire Post*)

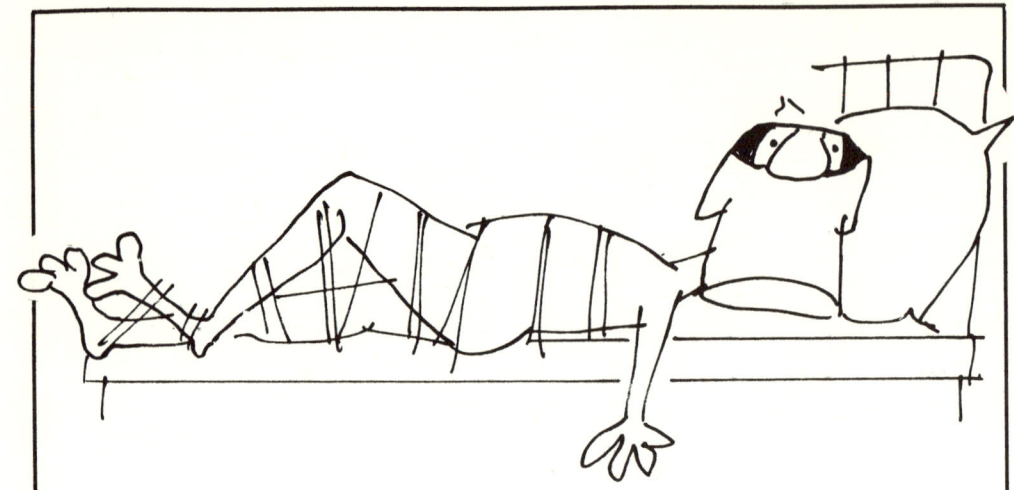

Police found a young man tied across Jessica's bed. "I broke in to steal a few things thinking no one was in, when suddenly I was hit over the head. When I came round I was naked, tied hand and foot to a bed. A woman kept trying to get me to agree to be her lover ... finally she got fed up with it and called the police." (*Reveille*)

A Warwick husband stripped his estranged wife, tied her to the bed, and poured boiling water over her after dragging her home by the hair. Then he told police, "I thought that by doing this she would see I wanted her." (*Evening Mail*)

One young woman I met said the immigrants had all kinds of perverted customs: they even made the women take off all their clothes before sexual intercourse. (*Observer*)

A Sporting Chance

Few things in life are more ridiculous than the pastime known as sport. A group of adults throw, kick, or hit a ball or puck against another group of adults attempting to stop the same ball or puck being hit, thrown, or kicked. Yet most of these are winners. They're paid for what they do. It's us who are the losers. We pay to watch them. Surely it's better to get out into the clean fresh air and work for the good of all creatures great and small.

A rare bird made an incredible flight of eight thousand miles from Siberia to Bermuda only to be shot on arrival by a conservation officer. Mr. David Wingate explained that he killed the bird so that it could be sent away for positive identification. (*Cruel Sports*)

Mansfield, without a win at Field Mill since September 30, tried a spot of pre-match psychology in a bid to end the jinx. Manager Billy Bingham took the players on a coach trip to give them the illusion they were playing away, where their results are much better. (*Nottingham Football Post*)

Scout Tom Dexter has won an award for sleeping in uncomfortable places for fourteen nights. They included a toilet, a coal bin, and a car trunk. (*Evening Post*)

James McWilliams of Newcastle was remanded on bail after being arrested on the afternoon of the Millwall-Newcastle game at Millwall and charged with damaging 240 eggs, three lettuces, and ten pounds of mushrooms. (*South London Press*)

If the Lawn Bowling Club committee had treated its seventy-four-year-old greenskeeper with more understanding, he would never have burned down their clubhouse. (*Observer*)

If foxes could hear all sides in the debate on hunting, I think they would vote solidly for its continuance. (*The Field*)

Mrs. Jean Robinson won the Jean Robinson Cup for the most wins. (*Westmorland Gazette*)

Private McNally would have beaten 2nd Lieut. Hoppe for the army cruiser-weight championship had he not so obviously suffered from an understandable psychological reluctance to hit an officer. (Letter in the *Sunday Graphic*)

Mr. Warwick's plans for a sponsored moped ride from Northampton to John O'Groats had a serious set-back today when he found his moped had been stolen. (*Northampton Chronicle and Echo*)

An obituary in *The Times* bid goodbye to a well-known squire: "But, if he was a sage in business hours, he was always a boy at heart. The heart was given to birds, beasts, and flowers. He was an eager field naturalist and gardener, a still keener shot. And like most great English killers of birds, he was a merciful man who cherished the victims he slew so cleanly."

At 11:59 PM on November 14, about eight hundred people will set off on a five-mile hike to the 762-foot summit of Ivinghoe Beacon, in Hertfordshire. They will carry with them aspidistras in pots, or objects and plants resembling aspidistras, to take part in the World Aspidistra Show. At the summit, they will compete in a so-called nut-cracking contest, which entails pushing a block of wood round a marked course with their heads in the pitch dark.
(*Evening Standard*)

Mountaineers plan to become the first in the world to scale the fearsome Stourbridge High Street. They will kit themselves out in full climbing gear and lie flat on the road surface. They will use lampposts, drains, and road signs as footholds. Said Mr. Len Scarlett, "Actually it will be quite a difficult climb, because there aren't many lampposts in the High Street." (*Wolverhampton Express and Star*)

The Care and Feeding of Losers

Even losers need feeding.
And it's not just what they eat.
It's where they eat.

The College of Arms once told an anxious hostess who sought its advice over the seating arrangements for her dinner party, "The Aga Khan is held to be a direct descendant of God ... An English duke takes precedence."

We apologize profusely to all our patrons who received, through unfortunate computer error, the chest measurements of members of Female Wrestlers Association instead of the figures on sales of soybeans to foreign countries. (*Saturday Review*)

The thirtieth annual Foire Gastronomique, perhaps the greatest food fair in Europe, has just ended here in Dijon. The British stand was displaying, among other national delicacies, tins of cat and dog food. (*The Times*)

"I felt the meaning went out of my life the day soup started arriving in envelopes." (Letter to *The Times*)

African frogs legs were off the official menu at an official lunch yesterday for visiting Gabonese President Omar Bongo, after Australian quarantine officers destroyed the president's twelve African bullfrogs found in his official plane.
(*Press and Journal*)

In view of the appalling harvest, I suggest that the normal Harvest Festival services are either suspended altogether or modified in some way to register our disappointment.
(Letter in the *Leicester Mercury*)

Corned beef was sent to a school canteen. Teachers sniffed it and did not like it. The canteen manageress sniffed it, but pronounced it good; the town sanitary inspector sniffed it and passed it as good; the town medical officer sniffed it and declared it good – then ordered it to be destroyed because too many people had sniffed it.
(*Daily Express*)

"On the first application it was stated that Taylor was suffering from malnutrition. We were advised that a person suffering from this complaint did not require extra rations, so the application was refused."
(*Daily Mail*)

Dog for Sale, eats anything. Fond of children.
(Advertisement in the *Hayes News*)

When I complimented the waitress on the high standard the restaurant maintained, she answered, "You'll never find any cracked crockery in here. Why, the moment a cup is cracked, it is sent up at once to the staff canteen."
(Letter in the *Guardian*)

On the Road

Driving a car is not my idea of fun. As Rodney Dangerfield said, "When I take my family out for a drive it's for a Sunday shove."

Despite that, we do own a car at present, and it has given us little or no trouble since the day we bought it ... yesterday.

A motorist who drove his car on the wrong side of the road and ran off when police caught up with him, refused a breath test on the grounds that he was a pedestrian.
(*The Malvern Gazette and Ledbury Reporter*)

George Featherstone walks three miles to work because a robin is nesting under the saddle of his motor cycle. (*Daily Telegraph*)

The driver was asked by a police inspector, "After the accident, why did you raise your hat to acknowledge the driver of the other car involved when you did not know him?"

The driver replied, "The accident had caused the hat to become crammed down over my eyes and ears and – although it might have been polite to raise it to the other driver – I lifted it to alleviate my discomfort."
(*The Advertiser*)

The trunk isn't very big, but a man from the factory warned me about that. He told me, "A Rolls-Royce owner's luggage, sir, should precede him by rail or air." (*AA Motorist Magazine*)

Student-driver Phillip Drake nearly knocked down a policeman when backing up his car. Drake told the magistrate that he had mistaken the policeman for a lamppost. (*Daily Times*)

The defence that a driver was not responsible for his action if he suddenly lapsed into unconsciousness was refuted by the sheriff, who said the case quoted did not include the fact that the driver had been hit on the head with a brick. (*Evening News*)

A legally blind great-grandfather was charged with running down a group of children. He thought his car had hit a garbage can. Sentenced to three months to five years, the driver said, "I think it's unfair. I had no intention of hurting the girls. I just didn't see them." (*UPI*)

A motor horse-box carrying a live horse can travel at 30 MPH. If the horse dies in transit, the vehicle immediately becomes a carrier of horseflesh and by law must reduce speed to 20 MPH. (*Daily Mail*)

"Garbage trucks are driven as though they were taking part in the Monte Carlo rally," the town councillor stated. "Old ladies are forced to run up the streets carrying their cans in pursuit of the speedy trash collectors." (*The Journal*)

The "fairly horrifying account" of a car chase in which police were in pursuit of a vehicle carrying a person on the bonnet was told at Aberdeen Sheriff Court today. Mr. Angus Reith described how the car travelled at 55 MPH and the passenger was seen hanging on to the windscreen wipers "rather tightly." (*Aberdeen Evening Express*)

Horace Vere de Cole was walking down the street when he spotted a group of workmen standing around, obviously waiting for their foreman to show up. Assuming an imposing air, Mr. Cole said, "Why are you loafing around here? Get your tools and come with me." Without a word, the men followed him to one of the city's busiest arteries. Cole then paced off an area in the middle of the street and told the workers to start digging.

Some policemen saw the activity and co-operated by diverting the traffic. At the end of the day, when a large section of road had been dug up, Mr. Cole dismissed the men and told them another crew would arrive the next day to finish the job. It took the authorities two days to repair and clean up the mess.
(*The Globe and Mail*)

The Body Count

Everyone wants their child to grow up to be a doctor.
 Why?
 They're the winners, that's why.

> I HAD THIS APPLE ON MY HEAD AND...

A founding member of the Irish League of Decency, Mr. Joseph Murray, is recovering from a heart attack in a Dublin hospital. The attack occurred after he watched a nude scene on Irish TV. (*Cumberland Evening News and Star*)

The doctor said he would not be able to get Mrs. Linger into hospital, but Mrs. Hursell would see a remarkable difference in her mother within forty-eight hours. "We did," said Mrs. Hursell. "Mother died." (*Evening Post*)

Some of these new drugs seem to be so strong that you have to be in perfect health to take them. (*To England With Love*)

"I'm sorry, sir," a man was told by a maternity hospital spokesman in September, "but if your wife needs a bed in March, it should have been booked ten months in advance." (*The Times*)

Aristotle thought sexual intercourse caused baldness.

A senior physician told the *Times* that it was often found that persons suffering from severe pains commit suicide to get "permanent relief." He, however, said that it appeared unnatural for a man to take poison while riding a rickshaw.
(*Bangladesh Times*)

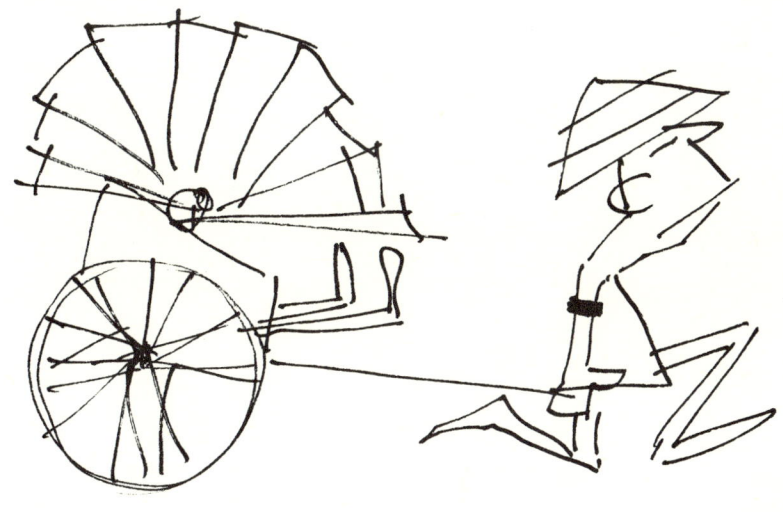

The word hepaticocholangiocholecystenterostomy may not mean much to you, but it means a lot to Mrs. Mary Alice Crossley (seventy-two) who is just recovering from one. (*Evening Chronicle*)

The loss of his eye bothered Lord Nelson so badly that he was heard to remark, "My eyesight frets me most dreadfully." This from a man who, when sick, would console himself with the words, "There, there, there'll be a battle soon and you'll forget all about it."

A recent study showed that the death rate rose when striking doctors returned to their normal surgery work-loads. (*San Diego Union*)

There were four of us in the doctor's waiting room when in walked a Pakistani. He was about to go straight into the surgery when a woman jumped up and grabbed his arm, saying in very deliberate English, "We are before you. You take your turn. Understand?" The Pakistani, in equally deliberate English, replied, "No, you are after me. Me doctor. Understand?" (*Daily Mirror*)

A railman entered hospital at Belfort for removal of his haemorrhoids and got his nose straightened. Dr. Jean Butzbach told the court, "It struck me that the middle of his nose was bent." (*Southern Echo*)

King Louis XIV decided to get rid of his toothache, so he had all his upper left teeth removed. The operation left an opening through his jaw to his nose.

John Calbert was training his German shepherd to use a gun to ward off intruders. He was reported in satisfactory condition with a bullet wound in his leg after being shot by his dog, Jarvis. Michigan police say that no charges would be laid, as "It'd be kind of hard to fingerprint the suspect." (*Detroit News*)

The Moment of Truth

Are you a loser? Just be patient. Eventually someone will let you know.

Noel Coward was confronted by a middle-aged female fan who began, "Oh, Mr. Coward, you don't know me...." He smiled sweetly and answered, "But of course I do. And how is Aunt Mabel?"

An English socialist minister was dining with King George VI. He asked the king if he would like a cigar. "Oh no, thank you," the king replied, "I only smoke on special occasions."

Lord Nuffield, the motor magnate, had dined at an Oxford college. A porter produced his hat rather briskly and Nuffield inquired, "How do you know it's mine?" The porter replied, "I don't, my Lord. But it's the one you came in with."

Calvin Coolidge was once approached by a young girl who excitedly gushed, "Oh, Mr. President, Poppa says that if I can get three words out of you he will buy me a fur coat. The president snapped back, "Father wins."

An aristocrat, exasperated by the slow service in the dining-room of his club, finally asked his waiter indignantly, "Do you know who I am?" "No sir," replied the waiter, "But I shall make inquiries and inform you directly."

That woman speaks eighteen languages, and she can't say "no" in any of them.
(Dorothy Parker)

F.E. Smith, Earl of Birkenhead, taunted Lord Chief Justice Hewart about the size of his stomach. Hewart replied, "If it's a boy I'll call him John. If it's a girl I'll call her Mary. But if, as I suspect, it's only wind, I'll call it F.E. Smith."

Winston has devoted the best years of his life to preparing his impromptu speeches. (F.E. Smith)

The wife of Chico Marx caught him kissing a chorus girl. During the row that ensued, Chico claimed,
"I wasn't kissing her. I was whispering in her mouth."

The mother of an obnoxious teenager told Tallulah Bankhead, "We just don't know what to make of him. Miss Bankhead replied, "How about a nice rug?"

A Loser in the Family

The mother complained that her son, an only child, was becoming truculent, had started smoking, had been seen entering a tavern, and was keeping company with a girl.

Inspector McCann reported, "I found that the son was thirty-six." (*Daily Post*)

So determined was I that my two young sons should grow up, their mouths unsullied by swear words, that I consulted a psychologist. He said that if I swore freely in front of them, swearing would cease to have any novelty for them and they would not be interested. He was right. My boys do not swear, but I am inextricably in the grip of the swearing habit.
(Letter in *Reynolds' News*)

How do you get into the minds of young people these days? I'll tell you how. My daughter broke a plant pot in her room a week ago and yesterday the pieces were still lying on the floor.

I had had enough. I borrowed a toy revolver from my son, and put on a mask. I forced her at gunpoint up to her room and indicated the job to be done. Instead of snarling, "Ya can't git away with this," she cleared up the mess and brightly inquired, "What's for tea, mummy?" (Letter to the *Daily Express*)

City Council yesterday took away its grants from two church homes for unmarried mothers and teenage girls and gave them instead to the Plymouth Dogs and Cats Homes. (*News Chronicle*)

What nonsense to suggest, as your women's page did last week, that the use of a pacifier is either unhygienic or a bad habit which could become hard for a baby to break. I have derived great comfort from my pacifier for over forty years, and find it gives much greater oral satisfaction than the unhealthy cigarette. It is also much cheaper.
(Letter in *The Herald*)

Crime

We have arrived at the thickest section of the book – the number of pages, not the intellect of those involved. Indeed many of those who decide to punch holes in safes or pass scruffy pieces of paper across the counters of banks are far from stupid. They spend their days in the south of France living the good life.

You will not find their names here. They are never written about. For this would encourage all of us to grab an empty stocking and throw it over our heads as we aim for the nearest till. We shout about those who have tried their hand at the crime game and have come unstuck. Some of these losers fare better than others. With a plonk of the gavel, away they go. Others are not so lucky....

A magistrate was not biased against a man he called a clown, an idiot, a ratbag, a nit, a clot, and a dickhead, the Court of Appeal ruled yesterday. The court said the magistrate had merely expressed an opinion he had formed on the evidence against Michael James Daley. (*The Hobart Mercury*)

Ronald White (fifty) was sent to prison for three months yesterday after four offences of being drunk and disorderly took his total for similar offences to 126. He told the court he couldn't go to jail as he was starting work next Monday at Vaux Breweries. (*Sunderland Echo*)

A lawyer argued that a witness should be excused from court. "In the first place, he is not very bright. Secondly, he is employed on important government work."

The commissioner was commenting on the allegations made by prisoners at the Lusaka Central Prison. "How can someone say that he has been beaten up by a warder, but when opening his mouth you find that all his teeth are there?" (*Zambia Daily Mail*)

An eighteen-year-old girl accused of stealing a jar of vanishing cream has since disappeared, magistrates were told yesterday. (*Western Mail*)

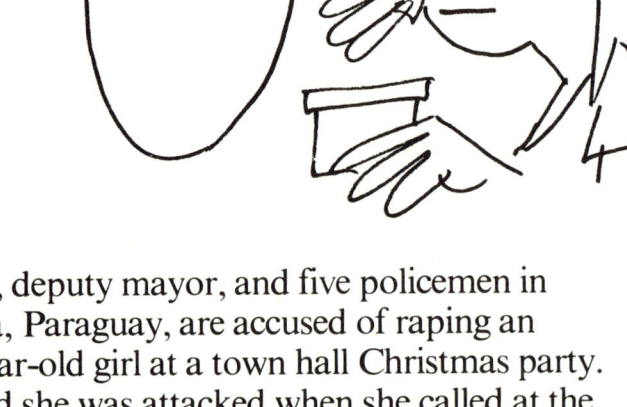

The mayor, deputy mayor, and five policemen in Santa Rosa, Paraguay, are accused of raping an eighteen-year-old girl at a town hall Christmas party. The girl said she was attacked when she called at the town hall to collect a good behaviour certificate. (*Daily Post*)

Nigel Pinn was walking in Railway Street when two young men jumped out of a van and began punching him, saying, "Is your name Mervyn or Malcolm?" When Mr. Pinn said no, one of his assailants stopped punching him long enough to say, "This is the third one tonight, we're bound to get the right one next time." (*Adelaide News*)

Police Constable Wayte told the court that the men pushing the wheelbarrow admitted that they stole the bricks. Thomas McDermott, labourer, said, "I was going to put them back when I'd finished with them." (*Gazette*)

Unemployed Patrick Foster spent almost $6000 in a week on horses, beer, and women. "I wasted the rest," he told detectives investigating a series of car frauds. (*Middlesborough Gazette*)

For the first time in Danish police history, a parrot has been questioned as a witness. (*Evening News*)

"I take the annual fancy dress ball very seriously," said Mr. Grahame Telly, after he was arrested while on top of a street lamp, dressed as a gorilla. "People dressed as policemen are as common as dirt, so when this man came up to me and demanded that I should go with him to the station, I took it as a joke." Mr. Telly, who was fined $70, offered to pay in bananas. (*Social Services*)

A judge reprimanded a witness who took the oath with one hand in his pocket. "Just remember, my man, that you are addressing the Almighty and a High Court judge."

Seats in public lavatories in Bath are being stamped with a secret code letter to help police recognize any that are stolen.
(*Sunday Pictorial*)

When a man with a handcart laden with bananas had to go to the police station for causing an obstruction, his customers followed.
(*Daily Post*)

A man was charged yesterday with using obscene language to a clockwork mouse that refused to perform. (*Guardian*)

The judge said the conduct of the defendant was disgusting. "That any man could hit a girl who wears glasses is beyond my comprehension."

When the Court was being modernized, the dock was built only four foot long. Only people under five feet can squeeze in. Officials have tried to ease the problem by making taller people lie along the bench. (*Daily Record*)

A woman's topless protest against her bail conditions flopped when the officer greeted her with, "Good afternoon, sir." The officer said, "She was rather underendowed, and had short hair." (*The Herald*)

Chong was visited at his home by all three and after various threats he was punched in the face, it was alleged. Eventually he decided to hand over $37, and Chow, who had punched him, gave him his change. (*The Gazette*)

A Halifax magistrate was told that a man who stole a jacket from a store went back and took another when his girl-friend told him the first was too tight. (*Evening Post*)

"In ninety-nine cases out of a hundred," said the judge, "a man who runs away is guilty, but X was the innocent one per cent. Mrs. Y had no right to shout, 'Stop that man' when he bolted. She should have called out, 'Will you please stop that gentleman, and kindly ask him to give me his name and address as he has just assaulted me.'" (*Mirror*)

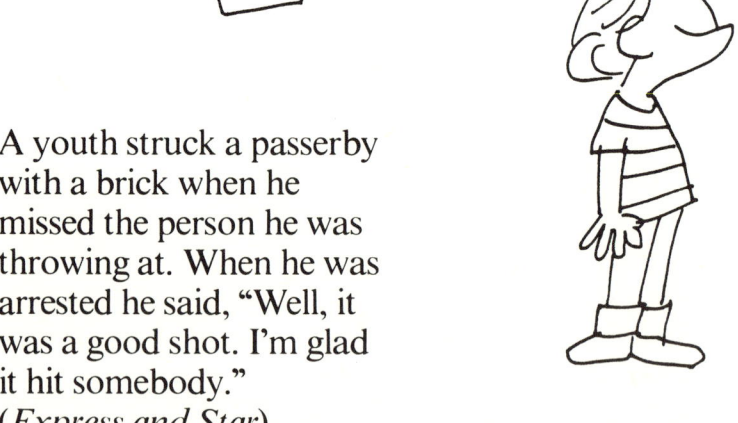

A youth struck a passerby with a brick when he missed the person he was throwing at. When he was arrested he said, "Well, it was a good shot. I'm glad it hit somebody."
(*Express and Star*)

When the victim regained consciousness, the attacker apologized. He then retracted the apology and threw the man downstairs again, knocking him unconscious for the second time.
(*The Western News*)

After being mugged three times, pensioner Richard Dalton took self-protection beyond its legal limit. The frightened old man was found to be carrying eleven knives, knuckle dusters, and a mountaineer's ice pick disguised as a walking stick. (*The Star*)

Golf caddie Leslie Gordon Waterman, thirty-two, was sentenced to nine months' imprisonment for stealing 126 golf balls and committing bigamy with Irene Harrop.
(*News of the World*)

During the last six months I have knocked over no fewer than four cyclists. On each occasion the cyclist was entirely to blame. In future I shall let them take the consequences of their own folly, and make no effort to avoid them.
(Letter in the *Sun*)

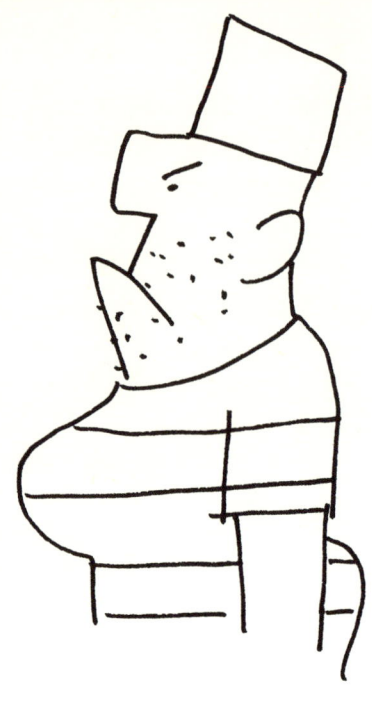

An illegal immigrant, said to be part man and part woman as a result of an unfinished sex change process, was being detained in a men's prison despite a lawyer's request for his client to be treated as a woman. (*The Post*)

When they were arrested at 2:40 AM Sunday, the men denied being near the premises with intent to steal. Both claimed they were looking for goldfish, although one did admit he would have been surprised if they had found any. (*Evening News*)

Councillor Hawton said many young people enjoyed beating old ladies, but that did not mean they should be allowed to. (*Rochdale Observer*)

Police are searching for the person who stole singer George Watson's suit. George is 6 ft. 2 in. and weighs 300 lbs. A police officer said, "We are looking for a very large man or several small ones. We are also keeping an eye on campsites in case it has been sold as a tent." (*Daily Herald*)

The lawyer played down the incident, claiming, "It is a perfectly ordinary little case of a man charged with indecency with four or five guardsmen." (*Guardian*)

In jail, Fuchs was put to work on kitbags for the army. Within a day he had calculated that by cutting cloth a different way, the Government could save several thousand pounds a year. He was given a five-cent-a-week raise.
(*Evening News*)

A man appeared before Macclesfield magistrates on Tuesday charged with causing over $50 damage by chewing the upholstery of a new police car.
(*Macclesfield Express*)

A man who was unable to blow up a breathalyser bag because it had holes in it, was fined $50 for failing to provide a specimen of breath.
(*Slough Observer*)

Christopher Chadwick returned to his room to find a burglar escaping through the window. The intruder dropped the television and lamp he was carrying and ran off. His solicitor said reports indicated that he had potential and that he had been offered a furniture moving job. (*Eastern Daily Express*)

The magistrate thought it proper for a man to beat his wife occasionally, and the Bible supported that statement. But the beating must be done as a service of love, not in temper. The accused should have used a reasonable-sized stick. It was a pity he lost his temper and used an iron bar. (*The Sun*)

A woman named her son Gabriel, but she always called him Sidney. It was not until he left school that he discovered his real name. He was so embarrassed by it that he refused to show his birth certificate to anyone, refused to work, and drifted into a life of crime. (*Brentville Examiner*)

A man who "rather fancied" a young bank teller wrote notes to her at the bank, serenaded her on a piano-accordion while disguised as a blind beggar, and finally appeared at the bank in tennis clothes and turned somersaults in front of the staff. (*The Gazette*)

An eighteen-year-old youth stabbed two people and then ran into a nearby police station to escape the pursuing crowd. (*Evening Mail*)

Police who caught unemployed man Ernest Downie on the roof of a drug store were told, "I wasn't after drugs. I was ripping off the slates to make a blackboard for my son." (*Express*)

Joe Basinger, a gas station attendant, was on duty late Friday when Larry Tate drove up and tried to rob him, claiming he had a gun in his pocket. Basinger refused to co-operate, police said, and Tate threatened to call the police to force him. The attendant offered him free use of the phone. Tate made the call and police arrived moments later to arrest him. Police spokesman Vi Troxel said, "I think we can chalk it up to his being a little bit stupid." (*Chicago Tribune*)

After successfully robbing old age pensioners, Cornelius Reilly complained to the police when he himself was robbed. At the station he was recognized from descriptions given by the old people he had robbed. In the line-up he was asked by an eighty-two-year-old woman where his eye patch was. Reilly stepped forward, put his hand in his pocket and pulled out his favourite disguise. "Here it is, missus," he replied." (*Daily Record*)

Police chased two youths after they saw them kicking a young man on the sidewalk. When they couldn't find the attackers, they went back to the scene of the attack and locked up the victim for breach of the peace. (*Evening News*)

Asked why he signed the confession, Clark replied, "I thought you always had to sign if a police officer told you to." (*County Standard*)

Dennard said he had decided to wait in the telephone booth until it was time to meet a friend. "I didn't think it would matter if I set fire to some of the directory to keep my feet warm," he said. "It had already been vandalized."
(*Evening Post*)

A Batley man riding a moped wearing tights and make-up and carrying a knife in his boot claimed that police picked on him because of the way he was dressed. (*Batley News*)

For the murder of policemen, prison officers, and security men, I would suggest amputations of both legs up to the body, plus prison for ten years, with no artificial limbs ever in the offing – only a small cart on very small wheels. That would be the main deterrent. Further violence, if any, could be dealt with by further deformities.
(Letter in the *Huddersfield Daily Examiner*)

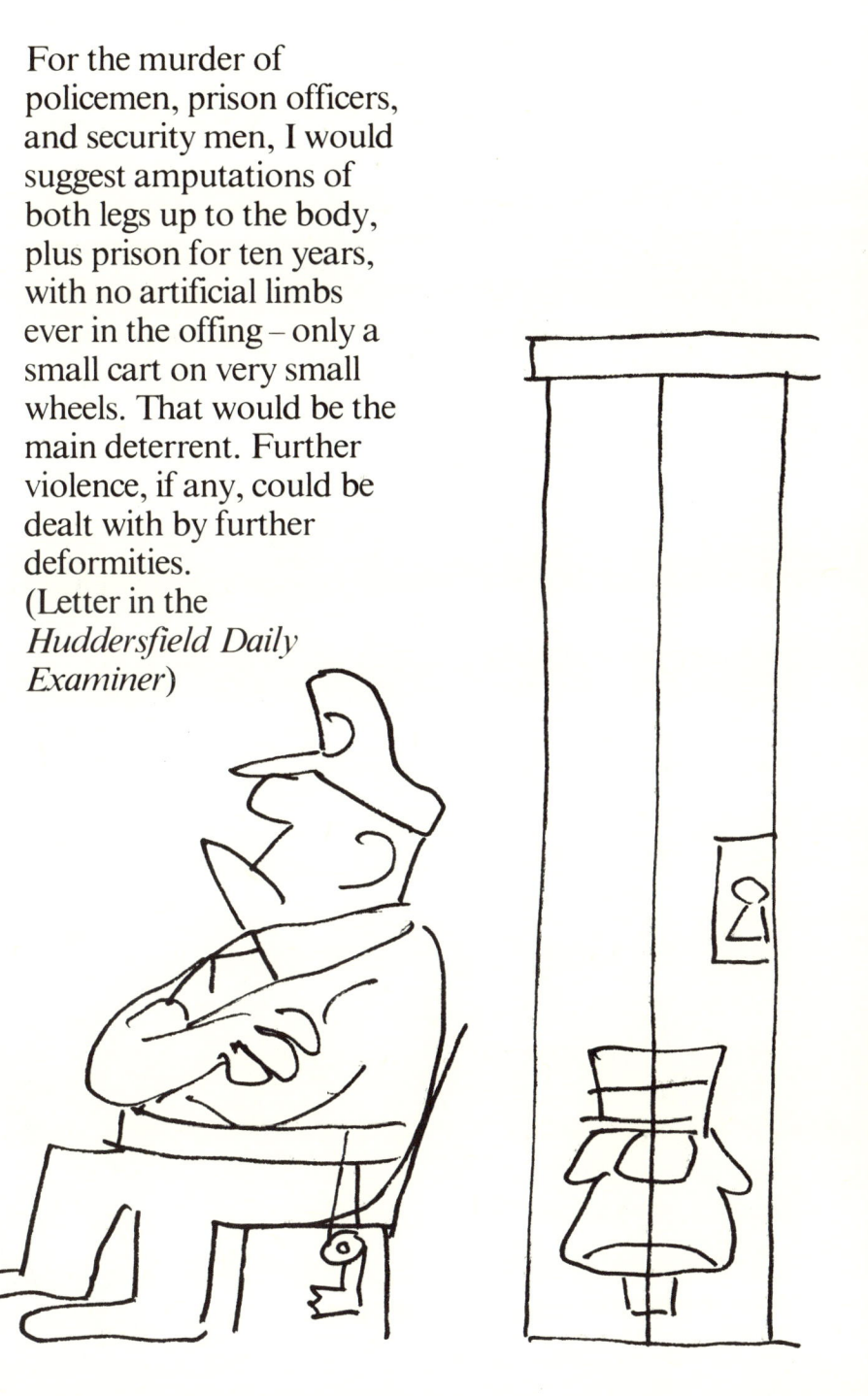

A night watchman was trampled by a wild hippopotamus near the Elephant River last night. Police report that the hippo "apparently ignored the man's attempts to frighten it off."

Asked if he could pay a $5 fine plus costs for maliciously wounding his wife with a poker, a man replied, "You will have to ask the missus. I have no money." (*Evening News*)

The woman said, "Three of my children went to reform schools for minor offences. Another was beginning to go the same way until I bought a television set on credit. The boy became as good as gold. He started to go to church after watching services on television, and would not go out even when we wanted him to. Since the TV was taken back because of non-payment, he has reverted to his old ways."

Having committed a burglary, Mr. Ealey was in such a hurry that he left his dog behind. When Detroit police arrived on the scene they ordered, "home boy," and followed the dog back to his master's house, arriving just minutes after the burglar.

Three men got stuck in the revolving door of the bank they were intending to rob. They were freed by the staff, who were unaware of the reason for their visit. A few minutes later, they returned and demanded $5000. Thinking it was a joke, the head cashier began to laugh. The men tried to escape, but got stuck in the revolving door on their way out. They were released a second time. By the police.

A man who could neither read nor write was found guilty of forging checks by Sandbath magistrates on Wednesday. (*Crewe Chronicle*)

The court was told that kicking down a pub door instead of attacking the staff was a sign of improvement in a boy's ferocious temper. (*Yately News*)

A telephoned bomb threat said, "Clear the school. We've planted a bomb." As it was 7:45 AM the voice was told that there was no one in the school until 9:00. "All right," the caller replied. "I'll call back later." (*Sunday Star*)

Dumb Animals

A visitor is coming to town whose fame rests on her ability to give birth to mice in her garage.
(*Ashbourne News Telegraph*)

Even in the flea circus times have changed. Flea impresario Alfred Testo reminisced "We used to get fleas from crane drivers' socks. Now, with all these disinfectants around, we have to advertise for them in the papers."
(*Evening Standard*)

There are few *Vogue* readers who have never harboured a slinking desire to be thrown across the saddle of a plunging white stallion, galloped to a palmy oasis, and stuffed with dates in a striped silk prison by swarthy warriors. (*Vogue*)

After a fight, a gorilla was rushed to hospital with a suspected broken nose. (*Evening Telegraph*)

The army came to the rescue last night, when they retrieved an old woman's cat from a tree. After being given tea and biscuits by the woman, the soldiers accidentally ran over the cat in the driveway. (*Cleveland Evening Gazette*)

A Moscow man has been sentenced to six years in a labour camp for trying to steal twenty parrots from the city zoo. The culprit was found hiding in one of the cages with the parrots in his briefcase.
(*Bolton Evening News*)

Although the owl was shot in flight, Ashton told police he thought the bird was a rabbit.
(*Manchester Evening News*)

The defence claimed that they had not intended using the ammonia against a human being. They thought they might run into a guard dog in the museum. Judge Block said, "I think the idea of using it on a dog is rather worse than using it on a human being." (*News Chronicle*)

A Portsmouth man believes he has found the way to talk to hedgehogs, although he does not know the meaning of what he says to them.
(*Evening News*)

NOT MINE – I THOUGHT HE WAS A FRIEND OF YOURS

It is because of unnecessary cruelty to worms that I would suggest the prohibition of all games on grass. I once saw a beautiful worm unnecessarily killed by a Rugby player's boot. Violence must be caused to millions of these useful creatures by the pursuit of balls. (Letter to the *Western Mail*)

As the seven hundred men taking part in the Freedom Parade approached the saluting base, a woman in the crowd noticed a caterpillar making a desperate attempt to cross the road. "Quick. Rescue that caterpillar," she cried. The man standing next to her dashed into the road and saved the tiny creature from certain death by popping it into his pocket. (*Hunts Post*)

I find to my delight that I can make my dog happy by wagging its tail for it. (Letter in *Reveille*)

I am a married woman, and I am fed up being stuck at home, and I wondered if you could help me as I am thinking of starting to breed with my poodle.
(Letter to the *Sun*)

Lost! Black, brown, and white collie. Answers to the name "Blue." (*Aldershot News*)

When rescuing a hedgehog that was being attacked by an owl on Monday night, James Cunningham, a Securicor patrol officer, was bitten on the forearm by a bat. (*Western Gazette*)

Police say they caught Vasquez and Evaristo Guedez red-handed as Vasquez tried to stretch the neck of a dog called Champion to make it look more like a goat. (*New Zealand Herald*)

...On With the Show

The Pigalle night-club will be doing its bit for politics on the night of the General Election. The line of chorus girls will be clad exclusively in blue, red, and yellow rosettes. Every time the Tories, Socialists, or Liberals lose a seat, off will come the appropriate rosette. (*Sunday Mirror*)

"We choose a number of men from the studio audience," said the manager of Quiz Programs. "We tie ladies' corsets around their waists, and the first to get their corsets off and hold them above their heads are put on the program. We find this gives us the right sort of contestant in a high proportion of cases."
(*Evening Standard*)

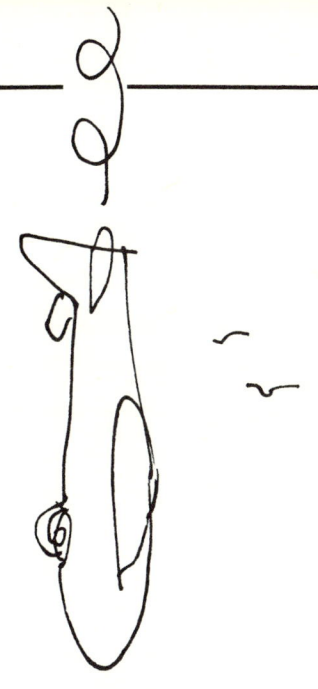

If for no other reason than sheer bulk, this book has to be taken seriously. (*Observer*)

It was regretted that the advertised event (free-fall parachuting) could not take place due to problems with the aircraft. But the most spectacular event of the day was the collapse of the beer tent. (*Daily Bugle*)

Police Constable Harry Powell, posing as a singer to get inside the Spare Wheel Club, sang "Goodbye" for club members, it was stated yesterday, when the club was struck off for serving drinks after hours. The prosecution said one man had to be restrained when Constable Powell sang. (*The Gazette*)

My own personal reaction is that most ballets would be quite delightful if it were not for the dancing. (*Evening Standard*)

Happily, in a week more full of alarms and excursions than any other since the Great War, we had an example of the British spirit at its best.
    Mr. James Whitehead, cellist of the Philharmonic Trio, faced with one of those impossible modern foreign compositions that delight highbrows, said, "Oh, I can't play this thing," and walked off the platform. (*Sunday Pictorial*)

KGB men holding a former Hull University student on charges of anti-Soviet activity have taken him to the ballet, the theatre, and the circus. (*Yorkshire Post*)

When the leading lady peeled off the last of her seven veils, she was revealed to be wearing a flared skirt and blouse. With sleeves.

Marie Theresa Regan (twenty-one), unemployed of no fixed abode, was refused entry to a dance because she was improperly dressed – she was wearing a boiler suit and rubber boots. When she appeared in the Sheriff Court she admitted assaulting a doorman by pushing a fish supper into his face. (*Shetland Times*)

On the wall of a building near his residence, director Mike Nichols noticed a chalk inscription, "I love grils." The next morning a line had been scrawled through this and a new line printed below that read "I love girls." The next day another line had been substituted – in letters twice as large. It read, "What about us grils?" (*Readers' Digest*)

The concert opened promisingly with Svendsen's "Carnival in Paris." In this, we were able to catch much of the authentic atmosphere of the Scandinavian fiords. (*Lancashire Evening Post*)

Owing to a girl's bashfulness, Brighton is without a Lady Godiva for its Jubilee Pageant today. A last-minute effort is being made by the organizers to find a girl willing to take the part. Otherwise, the white horse will be ridden by a man wearing flesh-coloured tights and wig of flowing golden hair. (*Daily Telegraph*)

In 1769, actor David Garrick decided to mark the bicentenary of Shakespeare's birth. It was held five years late and in the wrong month. A torrential downpour flooded the fireworks and none of them lit. A wall collapsed in the Rotunda and injured the main VIP, Lord Carlisle. As a Mrs. Baddeley sang the song "Soft Thou Gently Flowing Avon," the river burst its banks and flooded the tent. The dancers found themselves up to their ankles in water. As they left the tent, 150 fell into a ditch. As for Shakespeare, only one of the bard's lines was spoken during the whole four days, and it was misquoted.

On November 19, 1866, a Mr. Edward Falconer decided to merge the stories of two novels and present them on the stage. The play started at 7:30 PM. At 11:00 PM the audience began to doze off. Midnight came and went. By 2:00 AM only a handful of people remained in the audience. These were sleeping. At 3:00 AM the stage-hands held a meeting and decided to take matters into their own hands. Despite the action on stage they lowered the curtain. The play did not have a second night.

Playing Shakespeare is very tiring. You never get to sit down, unless you're a king. (Josephine Hull)

My weekly treat is a visit to a small local cinema. The manager there knows almost every customer. I have a seat booked at the end of the back row and, as I suffer from bad feet, the manager allows me the luxury of bathing my feet in hot water during the show. I fill up the bowl in his office. You do not get service like this in the big posh cinemas.
(Letter in *Reveille*)

Oscar Levant was playing a passage of Gershwin's "Piano Concerto in F" in a college auditorium when a telephone began ringing in a nearby office. Without interrupting his playing, Levant looked out toward the audience and said, "If that's for me, tell them I'm busy." (*Readers' Digest*)

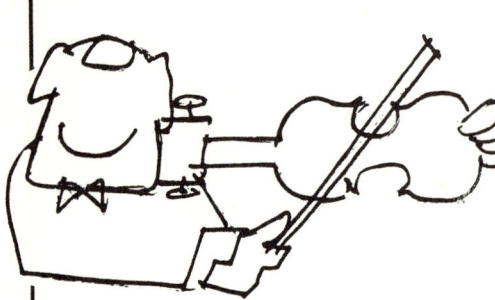

The Portsmouth Symphonia has been called the worst orchestra ever to perform in public. Two thirds of its members had never touched an instrument before the orchestra was formed in 1970. Before tackling any of the great symphonies, they agree only on when they should start and finish.

Mr. Jan Teigan made a perfect score during the 1978 Eurovision Song Contest. Singing a song called "Mile After Mile," Mr. Teigan was voted no points from panels of judges from around Europe. "This was my greatest success," said the singer after hearing the verdict of the judges. "I have done what no one ever did before me. I'm the first Norwegian to get zero points."

I know only two tunes. One of them is "Yankee Doodle" and the other isn't. (Ulysses S. Grant)

At a dull Broadway première, singer Margaret Whiting yawned, "I've seen more excitement at the opening of an umbrella." (*Readers' Digest*)

"Don't put your daughter on the stage, Mrs. Worthington." Noel Coward knew what he was talking about when he wrote the advice in this popular song. It isn't just the risk of runaway props and falling scenery. The real enemy hides in the audience, the ever-present critics ready to shoot down anything that moves.

"An amateur string quartet played Brahms here last evening. Brahms lost." (*Detroit News*)

"It opened at 8:30 sharp and closed at 10:40 dull." (Heywood Broun)

"My doctor won't allow me to watch Dinah Shore. I'm a diabetic." (Oscar Levant)

Walter Kerr said of an actor, "He has delusions of adequacy."

David Niven was an officer in the British army before he made it big in Hollywood. When World War II broke out, he returned to England and joined his old regiment. An old colonel, seeing him in the mess said to him, "Ah there, Niven, where have you been?" "I've been doing pictures," Niven said. "Really," said the colonel. "Water colours?" (*Readers' Digest*)

"I don't understand anything about ballet. All I know is that during the intervals the ballerinas stink like horses."
(Anton Chekhov)

"I played over the music of that scoundrel Brahms. What a giftless bastard!"
(P.I. Tchaikovsky)

"How wonderful opera would be if there were no singers."
(Giocchino Rossini)

Charles Lamb attended the Drury Lane Theatre for a performance of his play, *Mr. H.* It was a disaster. Although the play had been described as a farce the audience found nothing to laugh at. Soon boos could be heard and eventually the author joined in the hissing. Critic Crabb Robinson recalled that Lamb "was probably the loudest hisser in the house." Asked to explain, Lamb said he agreed with the audience. He started booing and hissing so that they would not think that he was the author.

At a performance of "Red Ridinghood," only two people showed up. To make matters worse, both decided to sit in the gallery. The cast begged them to sit in the orchestra, but they refused. As a result, the cast did not see a single person throughout the show.

"I have always said that I'd like Barrymore's acting till the cows came home. Well, ladies and gentlemen, last night the cows came home."
(George Jean Nathan)

And If Elected...

Guiding the team of ministers for the new premier is newly appointed Chief Cabinet Secretary Roksusuke Tanaka, a former journalist and Kamikaze pilot.
(*Far East Economic Review*)

A man who signed electoral forms with the name Kermit the Frog was fined $250 plus costs. He appeared in court dressed as the TV Muppet. The court was told that he had described himself as Mickey Mouse for the 1977/78 electoral register.
(*Evening News*)

Dick Tuck, an American political prankster, once grabbed a railwayman's hat and signalled for the engineer to start the train. It pulled out of the station with President Nixon still speaking from the back platform to the assembled crowd.

A British Member of Parliament was walking along with his friend, practical joker Horace Vere de Cole. Mr. Cole surreptitiously slipped his watch into the MP's pocket. As they turned into Piccadilly, Mr. Cole suggested that they race. As the MP sped off, Mr. Cole deliberately fell behind and began to shout, "STOP THIEF." The MP was arrested and almost forced to resign. (*The Globe and Mail*)

Thomas Jefferson said of the American minister to Spain, "I haven't heard from him in two years. If I don't hear from him next year, I will write him a letter."

Victor Biaka-Boda, who represented the Ivory Coast in the French Senate, decided to let the people of the hinterlands know where he stood on the issues, one of which was their lack of food. His constituents ate him.
(*Time*)

Lambs to the Slaughter

God is on our side.
Or is he?

Being asked the way to the workhouse by a needy looking man, I gave him a shilling. Judge my surprise, as a preacher and lifelong teetotaller, when he turned into the next pub, into which I followed in a useless effort to get my money back. What were my legal rights? (Letter in *John Bull*)

When asked her religion before taking the oath in court, the woman replied, "British." (*Evening News*)

The popular account of King John's financial dealing with Jewry is that he imprisoned wealthy Hebrews and had their teeth extracted one at a time until they yielded to his extortions. In all this, however, there are extenuations of King John. The government had to be maintained out of royal patrimony. There was then no comprehensive and well-ordered system of rates and taxes. Nor did he deprive them of the means of livelihood or cause them to be beaten up. His tooth-drawing was not sadistic, but a practical and comparatively mild way of exercising financial pressure. There was nothing malicious or destructive in it.
(*Church Times*)

Anxious to hear their grievances, the Bishop of London invited sixteen unemployed dockers to tea with him at Fulham Palace.

They produced their balance sheets showing that they received only 5d. a day and 2d. for each child.

"So I produced my balance sheet," said the bishop, "which showed that I received £10,000 and my expenditure was £10,600." (*News Chronicle*)

Losers at Large

There was a time when you could get away from it all. Not now. Even the shortest distance between two points has a bend.

British Rail are looking at the idea of improving the service between Luton and London by making more trains stop at Luton. (*Luton Evening Post*)

Because of new US customs regulations you will now be allowed to take only one bottle of whisky into the USA – not six as previously. The good news is that now there will probably be more invalid wheelchairs available for those who really need them.
(*British Airways*)

The Edwardians thought that vital requirements for travel beyond England's shores were, "Aspirin and quinine for fever, formamint and potassium chlorate for sore throat, veramon and pryamidon for headaches, bismuth and magnesia for indigestion, bromural for insomnia, cascara and Epsom salts for constipation, ammonia for scorpion bites, zinc or starch dusting powder for chafed sores, charcoal tablets and a body belt for diarrhoea, antiseptic wool, carbolic acid, boracic powder, iodine and corrosive sublimate tablets, and a clinical thermometer." (*Baedekker*)

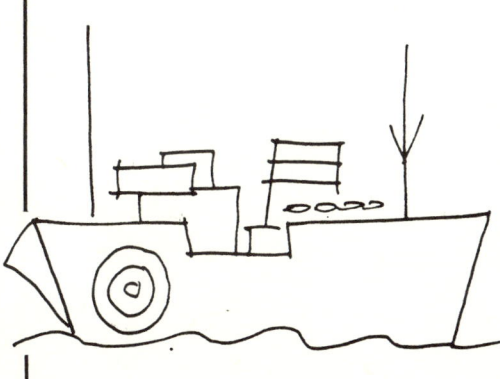

The bows of the *Napier Star* had ripped through the bows of the *Laurentic* just beneath one of the anchors. Three men were found dead in their bunks, and three others were missing amongst the tangled mass of debris.

How near disaster came to catastrophe was also evident. Had the *Napier Star* struck twenty yards further astern, she would have cut clean into the first-class staterooms. (*Orient News*)

"I wonder," wrote one man with time on his hands, even at the office, "if you could offer me some advice as to the type of plants which survive a hot, dry, dark atmosphere. I work in a large basement that has no window and consequently no natural daylight. A five-foot strip light is on between 9 AM and 5:30 PM each day. There are no external ventilators and the only means of obtaining any fresh air is either to leave the door open, or (for myself) to go and stand in the road for a while. If I leave the door open, there is an excessive draught and therefore I must keep the heater on all day. I have had no success in keeping and enjoying any form of plant life at all.
(Letter to the *Amateur Gazette*)

The late Lord Leverhulme remarked, "Half the money I spend on advertising is wasted; the trouble is, I can never find out which half."

For Sale: Gent's upright urinal;
also microphone, stand, and amplifier.
(*Buyer's Market*)

A wallet was found in a suburb by a German, who took it to the nearest police station. There he was thanked, asked his name, and detained for internment. (*Gazette*)

Apsley's first ever Community Day was hit by hazards when the hot-air balloon wouldn't go up, the ponies for the children's rides never arrived and the police display team were called away to the pop festival at Knebworth. On top of that the Judo Club didn't turn up and no one entered the beauty contest. Said organizer Mrs. Pat Jones, "It was a great success. We're going to do it again next year." (*Hampstead Star*)

Members of Ugley Women's Institute listened to a talk by Miss Wilson, of the Sue Eaton Beauty Clinic. (*Herts & Essex Observer*)

Old Maston has decided not to enter the best-kept village competition this year. Last year it placed fifty-fourth, and every part of the village, except the churchyard, was criticized by the judges.
(*Oxford Times*)

The course combines the fun of skiing with an opportunity to take part in language and environmental studies. On the cultural side, the trip was supposed to give students a chance to speak French, but this was slightly complicated by the fact that the resort was in Italy.

A New Zealand trapper lost in bush-covered mountains for three weeks survived by eating raw rats – which he made more palatable by pretending they were baked beans. (*Evening Post*)

Dr. Wearn has a great family interest in the Pacific. His great-great-grandfather, the Rev. J. Williams, was eaten by cannibals in the Solomon Islands.
(*Sydney Sun-Herald*)

People who find it necessary to vomit whilst in a railway carriage should discreetly use their hats. This would come naturally to anyone properly brought up.
(Letter in the *Picture Post*)

And when Miss Gertrude Usher went on a 1,300-mile weekend excursion by rail and steamer to the Inner Hebrides, she thought her time and money could have been better spent. When she got back to Euston, she said, "There was nothing but scenery up there."

Bea Lillie asked the question on one of the Queens, "I say, what time does this place get to New York?"

Mr. Smith finally arrived at Yarmouth today after hitting five other vessels and a floating museum. He denied using an AA road map for navigation.
(*The Star*)

When you're a member of the travelling public, there's nothing worse than getting burned to death in a motel room you've already paid for.
(*Morning Bulletin*)

The prosecutor accused train driver Somnuck Chaknam of driving over the 50 KPH speed limit while heading toward the station and blamed the mechanic, Ruen Porn-on, for failing to observe the green light signal, which was not on at the time.
(*Bangkok Post*)

Mrs. Jackson gets her knowledge of Arab tribes from living in the desert. With the help of her husband, she even built a house on stilts, though their belongings kept falling through the floor.
(*The Advertiser*)

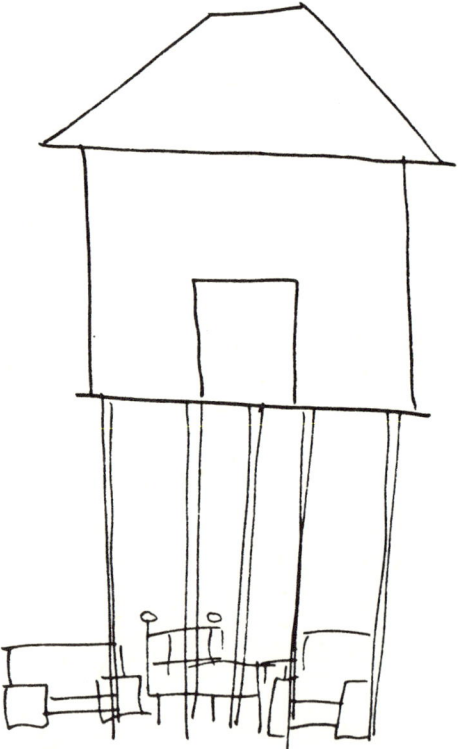

Help Wanted

Happy person with typing skills required for general office work. Hours 9 AM – 1 PM, approx., five days a week. A piano/organ player would be an advantage. Please write to Superintendent, Chichester Crematorium. (*Chichester Observer*)

Mr. Smith locks his alarm clock inside a metal medicine chest for extra noise. To open the door, he has to plunge his arm to the bottom of a deep jug full of icy water, into which he drops the key each night before he goes to bed. This is the only way he can be certain of waking up. (*The Gazette*)

They would not take on a young man for a job because it was so boring, management told an industrial tribunal – even a monkey could be trained to do it. They thought the job was more suited to a mature woman.
(*Public Service*)

Christina says she's taking care of some business and she will then be returning to Moscow. "I am here on business," she says. "I will then be returning to Moscow." Christina adds that she will be returning to Moscow after she attends to business.
(*Miami Herald*)

No one could have been more surprised to have been nominated "Best Speaker of the Year" than this year's recipient of the award, ninety-four-year-old Catherine Bramwell-Booth. "It was a complete shock," she said, "as I did not make a single speech last year." (*The Sun*)

Last night a store official said, "We have another Santa Claus now. We are sorry about Mr. Bates because he was so popular with the children. But we couldn't have him giving away toys."
(*The Advocate*)

If a 50-megaton bomb fell on Okehampton tomorrow it would, apart from spoiling everybody's day, pose a major problem for the Devon Emergency Volunteers. (*Exeter Express and Echo*)

The daughter of the Duke of Marlborough had her father as a house guest. She was surprised to hear him complain that his toothbrush "did not foam properly" so would she buy him a new one? He had to be reminded gently that without the aid of tooth powder, usually applied each morning by his valet, no toothbrush foamed automatically. (*Sunday Telegraph*)

The Burmese army and the RAF searched for three days. No trace was found of Princess Alexandra's teddy bear, although she told her host in Mandalay she remembered taking teddy to bed. Princess Alexandra is twenty-five this month.
(*Reynolds' News*)

Cannot the ban on the importation of parrots into England now be removed, thereby giving an opportunity for English exiles with their parrots to return to their homes for the Royal Jubilee?
(Letter in the *Daily Mail*)

The Palmer family failed in their great wartime ambition – to breed a red, white, and blue Victory mouse before the Second World War came to an end. (*Reynolds' News*)

Wanted young girl washroom attendant, genial work.
(*Western Daily Press*)

A middle-aged man rowing on Regent's Park lake tried to stand in his skiff for the Two Minutes' Silence. He overbalanced, fell, and stood waist-deep in water to keep the Silence. (*Daily Mirror*)

Though park railings in Manchester are being removed for scrap, the park gates will be retained and locked as usual at nights to indicate that the parks are in theory closed. (*The Dispatch*)

MP Mr. Ken Weetch today called for an inquiry into how the Arts Council gave a grant to three men to walk around with their heads joined together by a ten-foot yellow pole. (*Daily Times*)

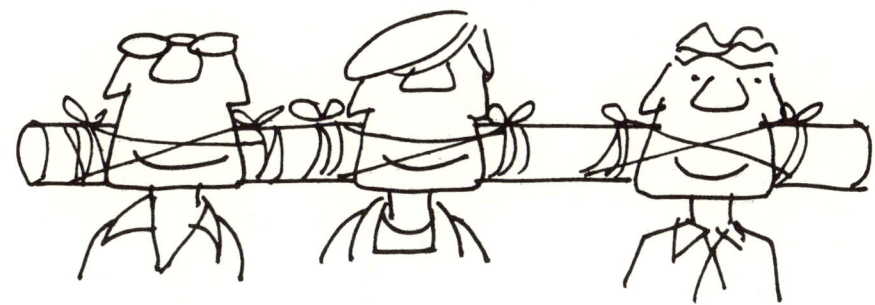

Lothian social work department is seeking the appointment of twelve extra staff to find out how many people are employed by Lothian social work department. (*Edinburgh Evening News*)

Your front page article about Africans being shot made me feel sick. Could not this kind of story be condensed and made more pleasant?
(Letter in the *Daily Mirror*)

"My party will continue to work for peace," said the politician. Hearing a certain amount of muttering, he added quickly, "But not in our time, of course."

A Dead Loss

You can't take it with you.
Be grateful.
Losers can.

Mrs. Minnie Day's landlord demanded four weeks' rent in lieu of notice when Mrs. Day vacated without notice. Mrs. Day had died.

For months, eighty-year-old Bert Jackson promised himself the first drink at a new club being built near his home. But a few weeks before the club opened he died. Today his widow, Mrs. Edith Jackson, will take a pint of beer – the first drawn at the club – to the cemetery, where she plans to pour it over Bert's grave to fulfil his wish.
(*News Chronicle*)

A Gainesville woman found dead in a Northwest swimming pool Friday was weighted with concrete blocks and suffering from multiple stab wounds. Sheriff's investigator John McManus said foul play is not suspected. "Right now," he said, "all indications are pointing to suicide."
(*Gainesville Sun*)

Farmer Obeid Abu Ali died at the age of 136 when he fell off the roof of his village home near Baghdad. Twice married, he left 170 children, the eldest aged 86. They were not all legitimate.
(*Yorkshire Post*)

She was a firm believer in "votes for women," anti-vaccination, and Count Mattei's electro-homeopathic globules.
(From an obituary notice in *The Times*)

As maintenance of the churchyard is becoming increasingly difficult, it will be appreciated if parishioners will cut the grass round their own graves.

Cemetery superintendent Frank Maule is delighted with his farewell present from his employers. He has been given a grave space.

Miles Johnson, a fisherman, said at an inquest yesterday that he had seen a man walking fully clothed into the sea, but did not speak to him because "in the past when I have warned people about danger, I've been told to mind my own business." (*Guardian*)

For Sale:
Gents black overcoat, long length, worn by undertaker, now retired, good quality, but one shoulder slightly worn. (*Post*)